The Chief Sinner Meets The Chief Saviour
Reflections On I Timothy 1:15

Joshua Rhoades

Published by Joshua Paul Rhoades, 2024.

While every precaution has been taken in the preparation of this book, the publisher assumes no responsibility for errors or omissions, or for damages resulting from the use of the information contained herein.

THE CHIEF SINNER MEETS THE CHIEF SAVIOUR REFLECTIONS ON I TIMOTHY 1:15

First edition. October 9, 2024.

Copyright © 2024 Joshua Rhoades.

ISBN: 979-8227082879

Written by Joshua Rhoades.

Also by Joshua Rhoades

Courage Under Fire: David's Stand On The Battlefield
Jonah's Journey: Voices Of Redemption And Lessons In Obedience
The Furnace Of Faith: 12 Principles From The Heat Of Faith
Whispers of Hope: Inspiring Stories of Men's Prayers In Scripture
Frontier Legends: The Oregon Dream
Elijah: A Beacon Of Boldness
HOOK, LINE & SAVIOUR - Faith Reflections from Fishing
Driven By Faith: Motor Racing Inspired Christian Life
30 Day Devotional - Bold and Strong- Coffee Devotions for a Courageous
Christian Walk
Authentic Christianity: The Heart of Old Time Religion
Consider The Ant - God's Tiny Preachers
Flee Fornication: The Plea For Purity
Renewed Hope- How to Find Encouragement in God
Sounding The Call - The Voice of Conviction
The Altar - Where Heaven Meets Earth
The Bible's Battlefields- Timeless Lessons from Ancient Wars
The Sacred Art of Silence - How Silence Speaks in Scripture
Under Fire- The Sanctity of the Traditional Biblical Home
Who Is on the Lord's Side? A Call to Righteousness
What Is Truth? - From Skepticism to Submission
First and Goal- Faith and Football Fundamentals
From Dugout to Devotion- Spiritual Lessons from Baseball
Par for the Course- Faith and Fairways
The Believer's Pace- Tools for Running Life's Marathon
The Immutable Fortress- Security in God's Unchanging Nature
Biblical Bravery
Deer Stands and Devotions: A Hunter's Walk with God

Dedication

To you, dear reader, who holds this book in your hands, this is for you.

Whether you picked up this book out of curiosity, desperation, or a deep longing to understand God's grace more fully, know that you are seen, loved, and known by the very One who created you. This book, "The Chief Sinner Meets the Chief Savior—Reflections on 1 Timothy 1:15," is not just about Paul's story—it's about your story. It's about all of us who, in one way or another, have wandered far from God, felt the weight of our sins, and questioned if we could ever be truly forgiven. We all carry burdens of guilt, shame, regret, and perhaps even a lingering sense that we've gone too far to be redeemed. But as you journey through these pages, let the truth of 1 Timothy 1:15 sink deeply into your heart: Christ Jesus came into the world to save sinners—yes, even the chief of sinners, like Paul, like you, like me.

This book is dedicated to you who are struggling to believe that God's grace is big enough for your failures. It's for you who feel weighed down by the mistakes of your past or the sins you're still battling today. It's for those who need to be reminded that the love of Christ doesn't shrink away from your mess but moves directly toward it. This is a book about the God who doesn't leave us in our brokenness but enters into it, who doesn't condemn us but reaches out to save us, and who doesn't just forgive us but transforms us, just as He did with Paul.

As you read, I pray you'll encounter the overwhelming love of the Savior who came for sinners. May these reflections remind you that no sin is too great for God's mercy, and no heart is too hard for His grace. The same Jesus who met Paul on the road to Damascus is the same Jesus who meets you today. He came not for the righteous, but for those who know they need saving, and His grace is greater than anything you've done or anything you will ever face.

So to you, the reader—may this book be a source of hope, healing, and encouragement. May you find in these pages the strength to continue your journey with the Lord, knowing that His grace is sufficient and His love is unending. This book is dedicated to you, as a reminder that you are not beyond the reach of God's saving power, and that in Christ, you are deeply loved, fully forgiven, and always welcome in His arms.

Introduction

In the heart of 1 Timothy 1:15, we find one of the most profound and life-changing truths in all of Scripture: "This is a faithful saying, and worthy of all acceptation, that Christ Jesus came into the world to save sinners; of whom I am chief." These words, spoken by the Apostle Paul, tell the story of an incredible transformation. Paul, once known as Saul, was a fierce persecutor of Christians, a man who sought to destroy the church and silence the message of Jesus. But something happened that changed everything. On the road to Damascus, Paul, the self-proclaimed "chief of sinners," met the Chief Savior, Jesus Christ. In that moment, his life was turned upside down, and the very one who had fought against Christ became one of His most passionate followers. This book, "The Chief Sinner Meets the Chief Savior—Reflections on 1 Timothy 1:15," is an exploration of the immense grace and mercy of God, a reflection on what it means for sinners—whether we see ourselves as "good" or "bad"—to come face to face with the One who can truly save. We will dive deep into the message that Paul shares, a message that is as relevant today as it was when Paul first wrote it. At its core, this book is about how none of us, no matter how far we may have strayed or how deep into sin we may have fallen, are beyond the reach of God's grace. It's about how Jesus Christ, the perfect and sinless Savior, came not for the righteous, but for sinners like Paul, like you, like me. Through the lens of Paul's personal testimony, we'll explore the transforming power of God's love and forgiveness. We'll see how the Gospel is a message of hope for the broken, a message of redemption for the lost, and a message of healing for the hurting. The idea that Christ Jesus came into the world to save sinners is not just a historical fact; it is the very foundation of our faith, the core of what it means to follow Jesus. This introduction is an invitation to reflect on your own life, your own need for grace, and to consider how the story of Paul's transformation speaks to you today. As we journey through these reflections, we'll be reminded that no one is too far gone, no sin is too great, and no heart is too hard for the love of Christ. His mission to save sinners is as active today as it was in Paul's day, and the invitation to meet the Chief Savior is open to all who are willing to come. Whether you are a believer looking to deepen your understanding of God's grace or someone searching for hope in the midst of your struggles, this book will encourage you to trust in the faithful saying that Christ Jesus came into the world for one purpose—to save sinners, of whom we are all in need of His saving grace. Through Paul's story, we will be reminded that God's mercy is not just for the righteous but for the chief of sinners, and in that, we find the greatest hope of all. Let us walk together through the pages of Scripture and be reminded that in Christ, we have a Savior who is willing to meet us, no matter how far we've wandered, and lead us home.

Chapter 1 – Proclamation

"This is a faithful saying" is a proclamation that stands firm, echoing through the ages as a bold declaration of truth, assurance, and hope in a world where so many things are uncertain. When the Apostle Paul writes these words in 1 Timothy 1:15, he is not merely making a casual statement, but he is placing a stamp of divine reliability on the message that follows, calling everyone who hears it to pay attention and trust in its unwavering certainty. In a world full of voices and ideas that often change with time, fads, and human opinions, Paul reminds us that what we are about to hear is eternal, unchangeable, and dependable. "This is a faithful saying" sets the tone for something that transcends the noise of everyday life, something that is firm in a way that human words can rarely be. It declares that this is not just another piece of advice or a fleeting thought but a truth we can anchor our souls to. The very word "faithful" carries with it the image of something we can lean on, like a strong rock that will not be moved by storms or waves. It assures us that the Gospel message is trustworthy, that it is something we can believe in wholeheartedly without any fear of being let down or deceived. Paul's choice of words here is deliberate—"faithful" means that this saying has been tested, and it has stood the test of time. It is dependable because it comes not from human wisdom, which can be flawed, but from God Himself, whose promises never fail. In a world filled with broken promises, shifting sands, and unreliable foundations, the proclamation "This is a faithful saying" invites us into a place of security, where we know beyond a shadow of a doubt that what we are about to hear is the unshakable truth.

When we think about what it means for something to be faithful, we think of something that endures, something that can be counted on no matter what. This faithful saying stands in stark contrast to the ever-changing nature of the world around us. People's opinions change, philosophies come and go, and even the things we once thought were solid can crumble over time. But this faithful saying doesn't change. It's not affected by the passing of time or the changing tides of human thought. It is faithful because it is grounded in the character of God Himself, who is the same yesterday, today, and forever (Hebrews 13:8). The faithfulness of this saying reflects the faithfulness of God, who has always been true to His word and His promises. When Paul says, "This is a faithful saying," he is reminding us that in a world where so much is unreliable, the message of the Gospel—the message of Christ coming to save sinners—is something we can hold onto with absolute confidence. There is no doubt or uncertainty in these words. They are a sure foundation for us to build our lives upon.

The faithful saying is not just a statement of belief; it is a call to action, a call to trust, and a call to hope. It beckons us to place our faith in the unchanging truth of the Gospel. In a world that often leaves us feeling lost or unsure, this faithful saying gives us something firm to grasp. It is like a lifeline thrown out to someone who is drowning, something to hold onto when everything else seems to be sinking. The faithful saying provides assurance that the promises of God are not like the empty promises we so often hear from people. God's promises are true, and they will never fail. The very fact that Paul introduces this saying as faithful tells us that we can rest in it, that it will not shift beneath our feet or change with the winds of circumstance. It reminds us that even when the world feels unstable, God's word remains solid and unmovable.

Moreover, the faithful saying does more than just comfort us—it challenges us to live our lives in response to it. Because this saying is faithful, it calls for our trust and our commitment. If we believe that what Paul is saying is true, then it requires something from us. It requires us to trust in the faithfulness of God and to live as though we believe that this message is the most important truth in our lives. It invites us to let go of our doubts and our fears, and to step forward in faith, knowing that we are standing on solid ground. The fact that Paul takes the time to emphasize that this is a "faithful" saying shows us just how important it is that we do not take these words lightly. They are meant to shape our lives, to be the foundation upon which we build our faith.

In a world where so many things are temporary, fleeting, or unreliable, the proclamation "This is a faithful saying" invites us to place our hope in something that will never fade or fail. It invites us to trust in the God who is always faithful, who has proven Himself time and time again to be true to His word. The faithful saying is a reminder that, while the world may let us down, God never will. His promises are sure, His word is trustworthy, and His love for us is steadfast. This faithful saying points us back to the heart of the Gospel message: that Christ came to save sinners. It reminds us that this is not just another piece of religious information, but it is the very foundation of our hope and our faith. This faithful saying tells us that no matter what happens in life, no matter how many things around us change or fall apart, we can trust in the unchanging truth of God's word.

The faithful saying is a call to believe in the faithfulness of God, to trust that what He says is true, and to rest in the assurance that His promises will never fail. It is a reminder that, in a world where so much is uncertain, there is one thing we can always count on: the faithfulness of God and the truth of the Gospel. When Paul declares, "This is a faithful saying," he is calling us to anchor our lives in the truth of God's word, to hold fast to the promises that He has made, and to trust that, no matter what happens, God's word is always faithful and true. This faithful saying is an invitation to let go of our fears and our doubts, and to place our trust in the unchanging, unfailing promises of God. It is a call to believe that God's word is true, that His promises are sure, and that His faithfulness will never let us down.

In conclusion, "This is a faithful saying" is a proclamation that reminds us of the reliability and trustworthiness of the Gospel message. It assures us that, in a world where so much is uncertain, we can trust in the faithfulness of God's word. This faithful saying is a call to place our faith in the unchanging truth of the Gospel, to trust in the promises of God, and to live our lives in response to His faithfulness. It invites us to rest in the assurance that God's word is true, that His promises are sure, and that His faithfulness will never fail. It is a reminder that, no matter what happens in life, we can always count on the faithfulness of God and the truth of His word. This faithful saying is not just a statement of belief; it is a call to action, a call to trust, and a call to hope. It invites us to build our lives on the solid foundation of God's faithfulness, knowing that His word will never change, His promises will never fail, and His love for us will never fade.

Chapter 2 – Precept

"Worthy of all acceptance" is a phrase that carries profound weight and meaning, especially when we consider its context in 1 Timothy 1:15, where the Apostle Paul proclaims this phrase to emphasize the undeniable truth and importance of the Gospel message. These words are not just an opinion or a suggestion—they declare something so critical, so universally relevant, that it deserves to be embraced fully, wholeheartedly, and without hesitation by every single person. "Worthy of all acceptance" means that the message of salvation through Jesus Christ is not something to be taken lightly or reserved for a select few. It is not just another religious teaching among many; rather, it is the ultimate truth, the foundation of all hope, and the greatest gift that humanity has ever been offered. When Paul says it is "worthy of all acceptance," he is urging us to understand that this message is worth our complete attention, our full commitment, and our unwavering belief. It's a message that transcends every boundary—cultural, racial, social, or generational. No matter who we are, where we come from, or what we have done, this message is for all of us, and it calls for a response from each of us. It is worthy of being accepted by every heart, every mind, every soul, because it speaks to the very essence of our existence and our deepest need for redemption.

In a world filled with countless ideas, opinions, and philosophies, it can be easy to become overwhelmed by the noise and distractions that surround us. We are constantly being told what to believe, what to value, and what to prioritize. Yet, in the midst of all this, Paul's declaration stands out like a bright, shining light, cutting through the confusion and calling us to focus on what truly matters. "Worthy of all acceptance" reminds us that among all the voices clamoring for our attention, there is one truth that rises above the rest—the truth that Christ Jesus came into the world to save sinners. This is not just an abstract concept or a distant idea; it is the very heart of the Gospel, the good news that has the power to change lives, to heal broken hearts, and to bring hope to the hopeless. It is a message so powerful and so transformative that it deserves to be accepted by everyone, without reservation or doubt. Paul is telling us that this message is not optional; it is not something we can afford to ignore or dismiss. It is worthy of our full acceptance because it is the truth that can set us free, the truth that can give us eternal life.

The word "worthy" in this context speaks to the value and importance of the Gospel message. It is not something trivial or insignificant; it is of the highest worth, more precious than gold or silver, more valuable than any earthly possession or achievement. To say that something is worthy means that it deserves our respect, our attention, and our reverence. And in this case, the message of salvation is worthy of all acceptation—worthy of being received with open hearts and minds by every person who hears it. It is a message that carries the weight of eternity, a message that speaks to the deepest needs of the human soul. It is worthy of being embraced because it offers what nothing else in this world can offer: forgiveness, grace, and the promise of eternal life with God. When Paul says it is "worthy of all acceptation," he is urging us to recognize the unmatched value of this truth and to respond to it with the seriousness and sincerity it deserves.

To "accept" something means to receive it, to take it in, to make it a part of who we are. When Paul speaks of "all acceptation," he is calling us to not just hear the Gospel but to fully embrace it, to let it penetrate our hearts and transform our lives. This is not a casual or superficial acceptance; it is a deep, wholehearted acceptance that involves our entire being—our thoughts, our actions, our desires, and our hopes. It means surrendering our own ideas, our own plans, and our own will to the truth of the Gospel, allowing it to shape and guide us in every aspect of our lives. To truly accept the Gospel is to recognize our need for a Savior, to admit that we are sinners in need of God's grace, and to trust in Jesus Christ as the only one who can save us. It is an act of humility, an acknowledgment that we cannot save ourselves, and a willingness to place our faith in the one who has already done everything necessary for our salvation.

The phrase "worthy of all acceptation" also speaks to the universal nature of the Gospel message. It is not limited to a particular group of people or a specific culture; it is for everyone, everywhere. No one is excluded from the invitation to accept this message. Whether we are young or old, rich or poor, educated or uneducated, the Gospel is for all of us. It is a message of hope for the brokenhearted, healing for the wounded, and salvation for the lost. There is no one so good that they don't need it, and no one so bad that they are beyond its reach. It is a message of grace that extends to every corner of the earth, offering forgiveness and new life to all who will accept it. When Paul says it is "worthy of all acceptation," he is reminding us that this message is for every person who has ever lived and for every person who ever will live. It is for you, and it is for me. It is for the sinner who feels too far gone, and it is for the saint who still struggles with sin. It is for every person who longs for hope, for meaning, and for a relationship with the God who created them.

In a world that is constantly changing, where so many things feel uncertain and unstable, the Gospel message remains constant and true. It is worthy of all acceptation because it is the one thing we can always count on, the one thing that will never fail us. People may disappoint us, circumstances may change, and the world around us may shift, but the truth of the Gospel remains the same. Jesus Christ came into the world to save sinners, and that is a truth that will never change. It is a truth that we can hold onto, even in the darkest of times, knowing that God's love for us is unchanging and His grace is always available to those who will accept it. The Gospel is worthy of all acceptation because it offers us something that nothing else in this world can offer—peace with God, forgiveness of sins, and the promise of eternal life.

"Worthy of all acceptation" is a call to action, a call to respond to the Gospel message with faith and trust. It is not enough to simply hear the message; we must accept it, we must believe it, and we must allow it to change us. This is a message that demands a response, and it is a message that is worthy of our full acceptance. It is worthy of being the foundation of our lives, the guiding principle for everything we do. It is worthy of being shared with others, because it is a message that has the power to change lives, to bring hope to the hopeless, and to offer salvation to all who will receive it.

In conclusion, the phrase "worthy of all acceptation" reminds us of the incredible value and importance of the Gospel message. It is a message that is deserving of our full attention, our complete trust, and our wholehearted acceptance. It is a message that offers us hope, forgiveness, and eternal life, and it is a message that is available to everyone. Paul's words challenge us to recognize the worth of this message and to respond to it with faith and trust. In a world where so many things are uncertain and unreliable, the Gospel stands as a truth that we can always depend on, a truth that is worthy of being accepted by all. It is a message that calls us to believe, to trust, and to surrender our lives to the God who loves us and has provided a way for us to be saved. This is a message that is worthy of all acceptation, and it is a message that can change our lives forever if we will only receive it.

Chapter 3 – Person

"Christ Jesus"—these two simple yet profound words carry the full weight of all that is precious, powerful, and redemptive in the Christian faith. "Christ Jesus" brings together the divinity and humanity of our Savior, presenting Him as the Anointed One, the Messiah, the promised deliverer of the world, and as the one who took on flesh to walk among us, to feel our pain, and to bear our sins. The title "Christ" speaks to His divine appointment, set apart and chosen by God before the foundation of the world to fulfill the ultimate purpose of salvation. He is the one prophesied throughout the Old Testament, the seed of the woman who would crush the serpent's head, the Lamb of God slain from the foundation of the world, the fulfillment of every promise, every prophecy, and every foreshadowing of deliverance that was whispered throughout the history of God's people. To call Him "Christ" is to acknowledge that He is the Savior, the one who came to rescue us from sin, to bridge the gap between a holy God and sinful humanity, and to restore what was lost in the fall of man. But when Paul calls Him "Christ Jesus," he takes it a step further, bringing into view not only His divine mission but also His human identity—the God who became man. "Jesus" is His human name, the name given to Him when He was born in Bethlehem, the name that would be called out by His mother Mary and the name He carried as He walked the dusty roads of Galilee, teaching, healing, and ultimately going to the cross. "Jesus" signifies His willingness to humble Himself, to step down from the glories of heaven and enter into our broken, messy world, to live as one of us, to experience hunger, thirst, temptation, and sorrow, all so that He could be our perfect representative, our mediator, the one who would take our place on the cross and bear the punishment for our sins.

"Christ Jesus" is the meeting place of heaven and earth, where the fullness of God dwells in bodily form (Colossians 2:9), and where God's love is made manifest in the most tangible, real way possible. It's in "Christ Jesus" that we see

11

both the majesty and the mercy of God displayed. He is the King of kings and the Lord of lords, yet He came not to be served, but to serve, and to give His life as a ransom for many (Matthew 20:28). In His title "Christ," we see the fulfillment of all the hopes of Israel, the long-awaited Messiah who would come to deliver His people. In His name "Jesus," we see the tender, compassionate heart of a Savior who would stoop down to wash the feet of His disciples, who would weep at the tomb of His friend Lazarus, and who would stretch out His arms on the cross in the ultimate act of sacrificial love.

"Christ Jesus" tells us that God did not remain distant or aloof from our struggles, but He entered into them fully, experiencing the depths of human suffering so that He could redeem us from it. He knows what it is like to be rejected, to be misunderstood, to be falsely accused, and to be abandoned by those closest to Him. He knows the weight of sorrow, the sting of betrayal, and the agony of physical pain. He is not a Savior who is far off, but one who is intimately acquainted with our griefs and sorrows (Isaiah 53:3). When we cry out to "Christ Jesus," we are calling upon a Savior who understands us, who has walked in our shoes, and who can sympathize with our weaknesses because He has faced them Himself. Yet, unlike us, He faced every temptation without sin (Hebrews 4:15), making Him the perfect, spotless Lamb of God who could take away the sins of the world.

In "Christ Jesus," we find the fullness of grace and truth (John 1:14). He came to reveal the Father's heart to us, to show us what God is truly like. When we look at "Christ Jesus," we see God's heart of compassion, His desire to heal the brokenhearted, to set the captives free, and to bring light to those sitting in darkness. Jesus said, "He that hath seen me hath seen the Father" (John 14:9), and in His life, death, and resurrection, we see the clearest picture of God's love and justice. He didn't come to condemn the world, but to save it (John 3:17), and in His every word and action, we see a love that is beyond comprehension, a love that would go to the very ends of the earth to rescue us.

"Christ Jesus" also speaks to the power of His resurrection and the hope that we have in Him. The grave could not hold Him, and death could not defeat Him. He rose on the third day, conquering sin and death once and for all, and in His resurrection, we have the assurance of eternal life. Paul tells us in 1 Corinthians 15:22, "For as in Adam all die, even so in Christ shall all be made alive." In "Christ Jesus," we are made alive; we are given new life, new hope, and a future that is secure in Him. Because He lives, we too shall live, and because He triumphed over death, we no longer need to fear the grave. The name "Christ Jesus" carries within it the promise of eternal life, the hope of glory, and the assurance that one day, He will return to make all things new.

When we call upon the name of "Christ Jesus," we are calling upon the one who has all authority in heaven and on earth (Matthew 28:18), the one who holds the keys of death and hell (Revelation 1:18), and the one who will one day return in power and glory to judge the living and the dead. He is the Alpha and the Omega, the beginning and the end (Revelation 22:13), and there is no name higher than His. Philippians 2:9-11 tells us that "God also hath highly exalted him, and given him a name which is above every name: That at the name of Jesus every knee should bow, of things in heaven, and things in earth, and things under the earth; And that every tongue should confess that Jesus Christ is Lord, to the glory of God the Father." One day, every person will acknowledge that Jesus Christ is Lord, but for those of us who have already accepted Him as Savior, we have the privilege of bowing our knees to Him now, of proclaiming His lordship in our lives, and of sharing His love with the world.

"Christ Jesus" is not just a title or a name; it is the essence of who our Savior is. He is the Anointed One, the Messiah, the Redeemer, the Lamb of God who takes away the sins of the world. But He is also Jesus, our friend, the one who walks with us through the valleys of life and carries us when we can't walk on our own. He is the one who hears our prayers, who knows our hearts, and who intercedes for us at the right hand of the Father (Romans 8:34). He is our advocate, our mediator, the one who stands in the gap for us, pleading our case before the throne of God.

When we speak the name "Christ Jesus," we are calling upon the one who has the power to save, the one who has the power to heal, and the one who has the power to transform our lives. His name is the name above all names, and it is in His name that we find hope, peace, and eternal life. "Christ Jesus" is the embodiment of God's love for us, the fulfillment of every promise, and the assurance that no matter what we face in this life, we are never alone. He is with us, He is for us, and He has made a way for us to be reconciled to God.

In conclusion, the phrase "Christ Jesus" carries with it the fullness of the Gospel message. It speaks of a Savior who is both fully God and fully man, who came to seek and to save that which was lost (Luke 19:10), and who laid down

His life for us so that we could have eternal life. It is a name that is worthy of all honor, all praise, and all devotion, because it represents the one who gave everything for us. When we call upon the name of "Christ Jesus," we are calling upon the one who loves us with an everlasting love, the one who has conquered sin and death, and the one who is coming again to make all things new. "Christ Jesus" is the hope of the world, the light in the darkness, and the only name by which we can be saved (Acts 4:12). It is a name that we can trust, a name that we can cling to in times of trouble, and a name that will never fail us. Christ Jesus—our Savior, our Lord, our everything.

Chapter 4 – Purpose

The phrase "came into the world" carries a weight of purpose, a mission, a divine plan set in motion long before the foundation of the earth, and when we hear these words, "came into the world," we are immediately reminded of the deliberate, loving, and sacrificial reason behind Christ Jesus' entrance into humanity's broken and fallen existence. These words speak of an intentional journey, a purposeful act where the Son of God, the eternal, all-powerful Creator, willingly left the glory and perfection of heaven and entered a world marred by sin, pain, and suffering. The phrase "came into the world" is not casual or accidental; it signifies the greatest act of love and mercy ever known. It wasn't that Jesus simply arrived or appeared by chance—He "came" with a purpose, a mission to fulfill. He was sent by the Father, as John 3:16 declares, "For God so loved the world, that he gave his only begotten Son." This giving, this sending, and Jesus' coming into the world was not random; it was driven by a desire to save, to redeem, and to bring light to the darkness that sin had cast over the earth. When we reflect on the fact that Christ "came into the world," we are reminded that He stepped into a place filled with sorrow, hurt, betrayal, and evil, not because He had to, but because He chose to out of His great love for us.

He came into the world knowing the cost, knowing that He would face rejection, knowing that He would suffer unspeakable pain, and knowing that He would ultimately lay down His life. Yet, despite all of this, He still came. The phrase "came into the world" tells us that Jesus was fully aware of the brokenness He was entering into, fully aware of the weight of humanity's sin that He would bear, but He came anyway. He came because we needed Him to, because without Him, we were lost, without hope, condemned in our sins. He came into a world that had turned its back on God, a world filled with rebellion, hatred, and violence, and He brought with Him the gift of salvation, the hope of redemption, and the promise of eternal life. Jesus' coming into the world wasn't just a historical event; it was the fulfillment of God's ultimate plan to rescue His creation from the curse of sin. When He "came into the world," He came with a singular purpose: to save sinners (1 Timothy 1:15), to offer Himself as the perfect, spotless Lamb who would take away the sins of the world.

The words "came into the world" remind us of the humility of Christ. He did not come into the world as a king in splendor or as a ruler demanding authority. No, He came as a baby, born in a manger, wrapped in swaddling clothes, dependent on His mother for care. He came into the world in the most vulnerable way possible, experiencing all the limitations and weaknesses of humanity, yet without sin. Philippians 2:7-8 tells us that He "made himself of no reputation, and took upon him the form of a servant, and was made in the likeness of men: And being found in fashion as a man, he humbled himself, and became obedient unto death, even the death of the cross." His coming into the world was an act of ultimate humility and sacrifice, as He exchanged the riches of heaven for the poverty of earth, the worship of angels for the rejection of men, and the glory of His divine throne for the shame of the cross.

But why did He come? What was His purpose in coming into the world? He came because we could not save ourselves. He came to bridge the gap between a holy God and sinful humanity, a gap that no amount of good works, no amount of human effort could ever bridge. Romans 3:23 tells us, "For all have sinned, and come short of the glory of God." We were lost, separated from God by our sin, deserving of death and eternal punishment. But Christ came into the world to take that punishment upon Himself, to die in our place so that we could be reconciled to God. Isaiah 53:5 says, "But he was wounded for our transgressions, he was bruised for our iniquities: the chastisement of our peace was upon him; and with his stripes we are healed." He came into the world to bear our sins, to carry our sorrows, to take the full weight of God's wrath against sin so that we wouldn't have to. He came to be the Savior, to offer His life as a ransom for many (Matthew 20:28), to shed His blood for the forgiveness of sins (Ephesians 1:7), and to open the way for us to have eternal life through faith in Him.

When Jesus came into the world, He came to bring light into the darkness. John 1:9 says, "That was the true Light, which lighteth every man that cometh into the world." The world was, and still is, filled with darkness—spiritual darkness, moral darkness, a darkness that blinds people to the truth of God. But Jesus came to be the light, to shine in that darkness, and the darkness could not overcome Him (John 1:5). His coming into the world was the fulfillment of the prophecy in Isaiah 9:2, which says, "The people that walked in darkness have seen a great light: they that dwell in the land of the shadow of death, upon them hath the light shined." He came to bring the light of God's truth, the light of His love, the light of His grace to a world that desperately needed it. And even today, that light continues to shine, offering hope to all who will receive it.

Not only did Jesus come into the world to bring light, but He also came to bring life. In John 10:10, Jesus says, "I am come that they might have life, and that they might have it more abundantly." The world, under the curse of sin, is marked by death—physical death, spiritual death, and eternal separation from God. But Jesus came into the world to give us life, real life, abundant life, eternal life. Through His death and resurrection, He conquered death once and for all, and now, for all who believe in Him, death is no longer the end. It is merely the doorway to eternal life with God. Jesus came into the world to defeat the power of death, to destroy the works of the devil (1 John 3:8), and to give us the hope of eternal life in His presence forever.

When we think about the fact that Christ "came into the world," we must also remember that He came not just for the righteous, but for sinners. He came to seek and to save that which was lost (Luke 19:10). He came for the broken, the outcast, the rejected, the hurting, and the hopeless. He didn't come for those who thought they had it all together; He came for those who knew they were in desperate need of a Savior. Throughout His ministry on earth, we see Jesus reaching out to the least, the last, and the lost. He healed the sick, forgave the sinners, touched the untouchable, and loved the unlovable. His coming into the world was a mission of mercy, a mission of grace, a mission to save those who could not save themselves.

But Jesus' coming into the world wasn't just about His earthly ministry; it was about His ultimate mission—the cross. From the moment He came into the world, His eyes were set on Calvary. He came to die, to lay down His life as the perfect sacrifice for sin. In John 12:27, as Jesus looked ahead to His crucifixion, He said, "Now is my soul troubled; and what shall I say? Father, save me from this hour: but for this cause came I unto this hour." Jesus knew that the cross was His purpose, the reason He had come into the world. He came to give His life as a ransom for many (Matthew 20:28), to bear the sin of the world, and to provide the way of salvation for all who would believe in Him.

His purpose in coming into the world was to reconcile us to God. Because of sin, we were separated from God, alienated from Him, unable to come into His presence. But Christ came into the world to make peace between us and God through the blood of His cross (Colossians 1:20). He came to tear down the wall of separation, to bring us back into fellowship with our Creator. Ephesians 2:13 says, "But now in Christ Jesus ye who sometimes were far off are made nigh by the blood of Christ." Through His coming, through His death and resurrection, we are no longer far from God; we are brought near, adopted as His children, and made heirs of eternal life.

Finally, Jesus' coming into the world gives us hope for the future. He didn't just come to save us from our sins; He came to prepare us for His return. Just as He came the first time in humility, He will come again in glory. Acts 1:11 tells us that "this same Jesus, which is taken up from you into heaven, shall so come in like manner as ye have seen him go into heaven." His first coming into the world was about redemption, but His second coming will be about restoration. He will come again to make all things new, to establish His kingdom, and to wipe away every tear from our eyes. Until that day, we live in the hope and the assurance that because He came into the world, we have been saved, we have been reconciled to God, and we have the promise of eternal life with Him.

In conclusion, the phrase "came into the world" encapsulates the entire purpose of Christ's mission. It speaks of His love, His sacrifice, His humility, and His ultimate goal of saving sinners and bringing us into eternal life. It reminds us that His coming was intentional, purposeful, and driven by His desire to rescue us from sin and death. Christ "came into the world" to save us, to bring light into our darkness, to give us life, and to make a way for us to be reconciled to God. It is a phrase that holds the weight of eternity, the hope of salvation, and the promise of a future with Him forever.

Chapter 5 – Plan

"To save"—these two simple words in 1 Timothy 1:15 carry the weight of the entire Gospel, the plan of God that was set into motion before the foundation of the world, a divine purpose that unfolded with every beat of history, every prophecy, every cry of the human heart for redemption. "To save" is not a plan of chance or an afterthought; it is the very heartbeat of God's purpose in sending Christ into the world. When Paul speaks of this in his letter, saying, "This is a faithful saying, and worthy of all acceptation, that Christ Jesus came into the world to save sinners; of whom I am chief," we see the scope and the depth of this saving plan. It wasn't a mission born out of obligation, but one that flowed from the immeasurable love of God. "To save" means to rescue, to redeem, to pull us from the depths of sin, destruction, and separation from God. From the moment sin entered the world through Adam, the human race has been in desperate need of salvation. Our relationship with God was broken, and no amount of effort, no accumulation of good deeds or sacrifices, could mend that divide. We were lost, enslaved by sin, condemned by our own actions, and facing an eternity separated from the Creator who made us in love. And yet, the plan of God was "to save." Not to leave us in our brokenness, not to abandon us to the consequences of our rebellion, but "to save."

In the phrase "to save," we see the very essence of God's character—His mercy, His grace, His compassion. God's plan was never to let us perish, though we deserved it; His plan, from the very beginning, was always "to save." To save us from the power of sin, from the death that sin brings, from the judgment that sin demands. And what is remarkable about this plan is that it was not dependent on our worthiness. The plan "to save" was initiated by God, not because we deserved it, but because He is good, because He loves us. Romans 5:8 says, "But God commendeth his love toward us, in that, while we were yet sinners, Christ died for us." Before we ever turned to Him, before we even recognized our need for salvation, God's plan was already in place. He saw our helplessness, He saw our brokenness, and His heart was moved "to save."

"To save" means to reach into the darkest places, the most hopeless situations, and to bring life where there was death. It means to restore what was lost, to heal what was broken, and to make new what sin had destroyed. The word "save" speaks of rescue, of being pulled from danger, and that is exactly what Christ did for us. We were drowning in the waters of sin, unable to save ourselves, but Jesus came and reached out His hand "to save." We were trapped in the darkness of our own making, blind and lost, but Jesus came as the light "to save." The depth of the word "save" goes beyond just a one-time act of deliverance; it is ongoing, it is complete, it is eternal. Christ didn't just come to save us from a single moment of sin; He came to save us from sin's entire hold on our lives. He came to break the chains of sin, to free us from its bondage, and to give us new life. His saving work wasn't temporary; it wasn't partial. When Jesus saves, He saves completely, fully, and eternally. Hebrews 7:25 tells us that "he is able also to save them to the uttermost that come unto God by him." "To save" means to rescue us entirely, to transform us from the inside out, to change our eternal destiny from death to life.

The plan "to save" is at the very core of the Gospel message. It's why Jesus came, it's why He lived, it's why He died, and it's why He rose again. Jesus didn't come into the world to condemn it; He came "to save" it. John 3:17 says, "For God sent not his Son into the world to condemn the world; but that the world through him might be saved." The heart of Jesus' mission was "to save." Every miracle He performed, every word He spoke, every step He took toward the cross was driven by this purpose—to save. When He healed the sick, He was showing the power of salvation to restore. When He forgave sinners, He was demonstrating the grace of salvation that wipes away every sin. And when He stretched out His arms on the cross, He was carrying out the greatest act of salvation the world has ever known. In that moment, as He hung there, bearing the weight of the world's sin, He was fulfilling the plan "to save." The plan that had been set in motion since the beginning of time was reaching its climax as the Lamb of God, perfect and without sin, took upon Himself the punishment that we deserved. Isaiah 53:5 says, "But he was wounded for our transgressions, he was bruised for our iniquities: the chastisement of our peace was upon him; and with his stripes we are healed." His suffering, His death, was all part of the plan "to save." And when He cried out, "It is finished" (John 19:30), the work of salvation was complete.

But the plan "to save" didn't end with the cross. On the third day, Jesus rose from the dead, proving that His power to save extends even over death itself. His resurrection is the ultimate victory, the final proof that He is the Savior, the one who has the power to give life, to defeat sin, and to conquer death. Romans 6:9 says, "Knowing that Christ being raised from the dead dieth no more; death hath no more dominion over him." Because He lives, we have the assurance that we, too, will live. The plan "to save" is not just about saving us from the penalty of sin; it's about giving us eternal life. It's about bringing us into a relationship with God, where we are no longer separated by our sin, but we are welcomed as children of God, heirs to His promises, and participants in His eternal kingdom. This is the fullness of the plan "to save"—to redeem us, to transform us, and to give us a hope and a future with Him forever.

The beauty of God's plan "to save" is that it's available to everyone. It's not limited to a certain group of people or a specific type of sinner. It's for all who will believe. Romans 10:13 says, "For whosoever shall call upon the name of the Lord shall be saved." The plan "to save" is universal in its scope, open to every person, no matter their past, no matter their sins, no matter how far they've wandered from God. Jesus didn't come "to save" the righteous; He came "to save" sinners, as Paul makes clear in 1 Timothy 1:15, where he calls himself the chief of sinners. If Paul, a former persecutor of Christians, could be saved, then there is no one beyond the reach of God's grace. The plan "to save" is for the lost, the broken, the outcast, and the sinner. It's for those who feel unworthy, for those who think they've gone too far, for those who are burdened by guilt and shame. Jesus came "to save" them all, to offer forgiveness, healing, and new life to every person who will come to Him in faith.

"To save" is not just a momentary act of rescue; it is an invitation into a life of transformation. When Jesus saves, He doesn't just leave us where we are; He changes us, makes us new, and sets us on a path of righteousness. 2 Corinthians 5:17 says, "Therefore if any man be in Christ, he is a new creature: old things are passed away; behold, all things are become new." The plan "to save" is not just about saving us from something; it's about saving us for something—for a life of purpose, of meaning, of walking with God and living out His will. Jesus didn't come just to save us from hell; He came to save us for heaven, to save us for a relationship with Him, to save us for a life that reflects His love, His grace, and His truth to the world.

In conclusion, the plan "to save" is the greatest demonstration of God's love for humanity. It is the culmination of His redemptive work throughout history, the fulfillment of His promises, and the ultimate expression of His grace. Jesus came into the world with a singular purpose—to save. He came to rescue us from sin, to redeem us from death, and to give us eternal life. This plan "to save" is for everyone, and it is available to all who will believe. It is a plan that was written in love, carried out in sacrifice, and completed in victory. And it is a plan that continues today, as Jesus invites each of us to come to Him, to be saved, and to experience the fullness of life that only He can give.

Chapter 6 – People

"Sinners"—this one word in 1 Timothy 1:15 captures the very essence of the human condition, a condition that every single one of us, no matter our background, status, or accomplishments, is part of. It is a word that humbles us, strips away our pride, and reminds us of the deep brokenness that lies within the heart of every person. When Paul says, "Christ Jesus came into the world to save sinners," he is not talking about a small group of particularly bad people; he is talking about every one of us. We are all sinners. The Bible tells us in Romans 3:23, "For all have sinned, and come short of the glory of God." This means that every single one of us has fallen short of God's perfect standard. We have turned away from Him, chosen our own way, and as a result, we are separated from Him, deserving nothing but His righteous judgment. The word "sinners" speaks to the reality of our condition. We are not just people who occasionally make mistakes or who are generally good but sometimes mess up. No, we are sinners. At the core of who we are, we are fallen. Sin is not just something we do; it is something that infects every part of who we are. Our thoughts, our desires, our actions—all of them are tainted by sin. The Bible even says that our hearts are "deceitful above all things, and desperately wicked" (Jeremiah 17:9). We may try to convince ourselves that we are better than we are, that we are not as bad as the next person, but when we are honest with ourselves and compare our hearts to the holiness of God, we are forced to admit that we are sinners, through and through.

And yet, in this simple phrase, "Christ Jesus came into the world to save sinners," we see both the devastating reality of our condition and the incredible hope that comes through Jesus Christ. Yes, we are sinners, but Christ came for us. He didn't come to condemn us or to leave us in our sin. He came to save us. This is the heart of the Gospel: that while we were yet sinners, Christ died for us (Romans 5:8). The fact that He came for sinners tells us something profound about the character of God. He is not a distant, cold deity who waits for us to clean ourselves up before He will have anything to do with us. No, He is a God who runs toward the broken, who seeks out the lost, who loves the unlovable. Jesus Himself said, "They that are whole have no need of the physician, but they that are sick: I came not to call the righteous, but sinners to repentance" (Mark 2:17). He came for those who are sick with sin, for those who know they are broken and in need of healing.

Being a "sinner" means being in desperate need of a Savior. It means recognizing that we are utterly unable to save ourselves. No amount of good deeds, no level of moral behavior can ever erase the stain of sin that covers us. Isaiah 64:6 says, "But we are all as an unclean thing, and all our righteousnesses are as filthy rags." Even our best efforts to be good fall woefully short of God's perfect standard. We cannot work our way into God's favor. We cannot earn salvation. That is why Christ had to come. The word "sinners" reminds us of our helplessness, but it also points us to the one who came to rescue us. Jesus didn't come into the world to be a great moral teacher or a spiritual guide. He came to save sinners, to do for us what we could never do for ourselves. He came to take our place, to bear the punishment that we deserve, and to offer us the free gift of salvation through His death and resurrection.

When Paul calls himself the "chief" of sinners in 1 Timothy 1:15, he is acknowledging the depth of his own sin. This is the same Paul who had once persecuted the church, who had been responsible for the imprisonment and death of Christians. If anyone knew the weight of sin, it was Paul. And yet, he speaks these words not with despair, but with a deep sense of gratitude and amazement at the grace of God. Paul's admission that he is the chief of sinners is not a confession of hopelessness; it is a testimony to the boundless mercy of God. If God can save someone like Paul, then He can save anyone. There is no one too far gone, no sin too great, that is beyond the reach of God's grace. The word "sinners" does not just describe the hopelessness of our condition; it highlights the greatness of God's love. Jesus came for sinners, for people who had nothing to offer Him in return, for people who had rebelled against Him and rejected Him. And He came, not begrudgingly, but out of a deep and overwhelming love.

The fact that we are sinners should humble us. It should strip away any sense of self-righteousness or pride. We are not better than anyone else. We all stand on level ground before the cross. Whether we have lived relatively moral lives or have fallen into the deepest pits of sin, we are all sinners in need of the same grace. This truth should also fill us with compassion for others. When we recognize that we are sinners saved by grace, it becomes impossible to look down on anyone else. We realize that we are all in the same boat, all in need of the same Savior. There is no room for judgment or condemnation, only for love and grace, because that is what we have received from Christ.

"Sinners" also reminds us that salvation is not something we can achieve on our own. It is a gift. Ephesians 2:8-9 says, "For by grace are ye saved through faith; and that not of yourselves: it is the gift of God: not of works, lest any man should boast." As sinners, we come to God with nothing in our hands, nothing to offer but our brokenness and our need. And yet, in His great love, He offers us everything—salvation, forgiveness, and eternal life. The word "sinners" may sound harsh, but in the context of the Gospel, it is a word filled with hope. Because Jesus came to save sinners, we know that no matter how great our sin, His grace is greater. No matter how deep our guilt, His forgiveness runs deeper. The cross stands as the ultimate demonstration of God's love for sinners, as the place where our sin was dealt with once and for all. Jesus, the sinless Son of God, took upon Himself the punishment that we deserved, so that we could be forgiven and reconciled to God.

Being a sinner means that we cannot fix ourselves, but it also means that we are exactly the kind of people Jesus came to save. In Luke 15, Jesus tells the parable of the lost sheep, where the shepherd leaves the ninety-nine sheep in the open country to go after the one that is lost. That lost sheep represents us—sinners, lost and helpless, unable to find our way back to God. And yet, Jesus, the Good Shepherd, goes after us. He pursues us with His love, and when He finds us, He carries us home on His shoulders, rejoicing. This is the heart of God toward sinners. He doesn't wait for us to clean ourselves up or find our way back to Him. He comes after us, seeking and saving the lost.

In conclusion, the word "sinners" in 1 Timothy 1:15 is a powerful reminder of both our desperate need for salvation and the incredible grace of God. It speaks to the reality of our brokenness, our rebellion, and our helplessness, but it also points us to the Savior who came to rescue us. Jesus came into the world to save sinners, and that includes every one of us. No matter how great our sin, His grace is greater. No matter how far we have wandered, He is willing to bring us back. As sinners, we are the reason He came. We are the ones He came to save.

And in that, we find the greatest hope, the greatest joy, and the greatest love that the world has ever known.

Chapter 7 – Pardon

"To save sinners"—these three words, so simple yet so powerful, contain the heart of the Gospel and the core of God's plan for humanity. In 1 Timothy 1:15, when Paul says, "This is a faithful saying, and worthy of all acceptation, that Christ Jesus came into the world to save sinners," he is proclaiming the greatest act of mercy, love, and grace that the world has ever known. At the center of this phrase lies the promise of pardon, the divine act of forgiveness that wipes away the guilt and shame of sin, leaving us free, redeemed, and reconciled to God. The words "to save sinners" remind us that salvation is not just about being rescued from a difficult situation or avoiding punishment; it is about being forgiven, cleansed, and restored to a right relationship with our Creator. When Jesus came to "save sinners," He came to bring pardon, a complete and total forgiveness of all the wrongs we have done, no matter how great or small they may be. Sin, by its very nature, separates us from God, bringing guilt and shame, creating a chasm that we cannot cross on our own. But the beauty of Christ's mission, as captured in this phrase, "to save sinners," is that He didn't wait for us to fix ourselves. He didn't wait for us to make ourselves worthy of forgiveness. He came to us in our brokenness, in our rebellion, and in our darkest moments, offering us the free gift of salvation, the ultimate act of pardon that only He could give.

The act of saving sinners is, at its core, an act of forgiveness. It is God looking at us in our sin, in all the ways we've fallen short, and saying, "I forgive you." It is a pardon that we could never earn, never deserve, but that is given to us freely because of God's great love for us. Isaiah 1:18 says, "Come now, and let us reason together, saith the Lord: though your sins be as scarlet, they shall be as white as snow; though they be red like crimson, they shall be as wool." This is the power of pardon, the promise that no matter how deep our sin runs, no matter how stained our souls may feel, Christ's saving work washes us clean. "To save sinners" is the declaration that Jesus bore the weight of our sin on the cross, taking upon Himself the punishment that we deserved so that we could be forgiven, so that we could be free. The guilt and shame that once weighed us down are lifted, replaced by the peace that comes from knowing we are no longer condemned, no longer defined by our past mistakes. Romans 8:1 says, "There is therefore now no condemnation to them which are in Christ Jesus." This is what it means to be saved—it means to be pardoned, to be released from the burden of sin and set free to live a new life in Christ.

In today's society, where guilt and shame can weigh heavily on people's hearts, the message of pardon, of forgiveness through Christ, is one of the most freeing and life-changing truths we can offer. We live in a world that often tells us we must earn our worth, that we must be perfect, that our mistakes define us. But the message of the Gospel is the exact opposite. "To save sinners" means that we don't have to carry the weight of our guilt anymore. Jesus has already carried it for us. The forgiveness He offers is complete; it is final. It is not conditional on our ability to make up for our sins or to live a perfect life. It is given freely to all who believe in Him, no matter how great their sin may be. This truth is like a breath of fresh air to a soul weighed down by shame. It is the promise that no matter what we have done, no matter how far we have fallen, there is always hope, always forgiveness, always a way back to God through Jesus Christ.

The pardon that comes with salvation is not just a one-time event; it is a continual reality for those who have placed their faith in Christ. We are not just forgiven once and left to figure things out on our own. Christ's saving work covers all our sins—past, present, and future. Every time we stumble, every time we fall short, His grace is there to pick us up, to forgive us again, and to set us back on the path of righteousness. 1 John 1:9 reminds us, "If we confess our sins, he is faithful and just to forgive us our sins, and to cleanse us from all unrighteousness." This is the ongoing work of pardon in the life of a believer, the daily experience of God's grace and mercy as we walk with Him.

The phrase "to save sinners" also reminds us that this pardon is available to everyone. It is not reserved for the righteous, the religious, or those who seem to have their lives together. Jesus came for the broken, the lost, the outcasts, and the sinners. He came for those who know they have messed up, who know they need forgiveness. His arms are open wide to all who will come to Him in faith, no matter how far they have strayed. This is the inclusiveness of the Gospel—the fact that salvation is available to "whosoever believeth" (John 3:16). No one is beyond the reach of God's saving grace. No sin is too great, no life too messed up for Christ to redeem. This is the beauty of pardon: it is available to all, without exception. All it requires is for us to acknowledge our need, to confess our sin, and to place our trust in Jesus, the one who came "to save sinners."

The pardon that Christ offers is also deeply personal. It is not just a general offer of forgiveness to the world, but a specific, individual act of grace toward each one of us. When we come to Christ, we don't just receive some abstract form of salvation; we receive a personal Savior who knows us by name, who knows every detail of our lives, and who forgives us personally. The forgiveness we receive is not distant or impersonal; it is intimate, relational, and transformative. When Jesus pardons us, He doesn't just wipe the slate clean and leave us to continue as we were. He transforms us from the inside out, giving us new hearts, new desires, and a new identity as children of God. 2 Corinthians 5:17 tells us, "Therefore if any man be in Christ, he is a new creature: old things are passed away; behold, all things are become new." This is the power of pardon—to not only forgive, but to make us new, to free us from the chains of sin and to give us a new life in Christ.

The forgiveness that comes with salvation is also full of hope. When we are pardoned by Christ, we are not just forgiven for the sins of the past; we are given the promise of eternal life. The act of saving sinners is not just about dealing with the here and now; it is about securing our future with God forever. Jesus said in John 10:28, "And I give unto them eternal life; and they shall never perish, neither shall any man pluck them out of my hand." The pardon we receive through Christ is eternal; it cannot be taken away. It is a promise that we will be with Him forever, that the guilt and shame of our sin will never again separate us from the love of God. This is the ultimate hope of the Gospel—the promise that, because of Christ's saving work, we have been reconciled to God and will spend eternity in His presence.

The phrase "to save sinners" is also a call to share this message of pardon with the world. Just as we have been forgiven, we are called to extend that same forgiveness to others. We are called to be ambassadors of Christ, sharing the good news of His saving grace with those who are still living under the weight of guilt and shame. In a world that is desperate for hope, desperate for forgiveness, we have the privilege of pointing people to the one who came "to save sinners." We have the opportunity to offer the same grace and mercy that we have received, to tell others that there is hope, that there is forgiveness, that there is a way out of the darkness through Jesus Christ.

In conclusion, the phrase "to save sinners" in 1 Timothy 1:15 encapsulates the heart of the Gospel—the message of pardon, forgiveness, and redemption that is available to all through Jesus Christ. It reminds us of our own need for salvation, our own desperate condition as sinners, but it also points us to the incredible grace of God, who sent His Son into the world to save us. This pardon is complete, it is free, and it is available to everyone who will come to Christ in faith. In a world where guilt and shame can weigh heavily on our hearts, the message of forgiveness through Christ is the most freeing and life-changing truth we can offer. It is a message of hope, of peace, and of eternal life. Jesus came "to save sinners," and in doing so, He offers us the greatest gift of all—the gift of pardon, the gift of salvation, the gift of a new life in Him.

Chapter 8 – Position

"Of whom I am chief"—these five words spoken by the Apostle Paul in 1 Timothy 1:15 carry an extraordinary weight of humility, honesty, and self-awareness. When Paul, one of the greatest apostles, refers to himself as the "chief" of sinners, he takes a position of deep humility, recognizing the depth of his own sinfulness. Despite his towering accomplishments for the Gospel, the miracles he witnessed, the churches he planted, and the souls he led to Christ, Paul never lost sight of where he came from or who he was before Christ found him. He was once Saul, the persecutor of Christians, the man who sought to destroy the church and drag believers to prison, complicit in the death of Stephen, one of the first Christian martyrs. Paul never forgot that he was once an enemy of Christ, and it is in that recognition that he calls himself the "chief" of sinners. Paul's confession is not one of false humility or exaggeration; it is an honest reflection of a man who has come face to face with the holiness of God and, in that light, sees the full measure of his unworthiness. Paul's position as the chief of sinners is not just about his past actions but about the condition of his heart. He understood that sin wasn't just about outward deeds; it was about the inner rebellion of the heart, the selfishness, pride, and rejection of God's authority that plagued all humanity. In seeing himself as the chief of sinners, Paul was not comparing himself to others in a way that minimized their sin, but rather, he was acknowledging the depth of his own brokenness before God.

When Paul says "of whom I am chief," he sets himself as the foremost among sinners, but in doing so, he also points to the immense grace and mercy of God. For if the chief of sinners can be saved, then surely there is hope for all of us. Paul's statement, far from being one of despair, is a declaration of the limitless grace of God. The chief of sinners has been forgiven, redeemed, and transformed, not because of anything Paul did to earn it, but because of Christ's sacrificial love. Paul's position as the chief of sinners serves as a reminder that no one is beyond the reach of God's grace. No matter how far we've fallen, no matter how deep our sin, God's grace is deeper still. Paul's life is a testimony to the fact that God's love is not reserved for the righteous or the morally upright, but for sinners, for those who are broken, lost, and in desperate need of a Savior.

In calling himself the chief of sinners, Paul also invites us to examine our own hearts. It is easy to look at others and feel that we are not as sinful as they are, to measure our righteousness by comparing ourselves to those who we think are worse. But Paul's example shows us that true humility comes from recognizing that before a holy God, we are all sinners, deserving of judgment. The more we grow in our understanding of God's holiness, the more we realize just how far we fall short. Like Paul, we too must take the position of being the chief of sinners, not because we are competing for the title, but because when we truly grasp the depth of our sin, we understand that our need for God's grace is as great as anyone else's.

Paul's statement "of whom I am chief" also speaks to the ongoing nature of our struggle with sin. Even after we are saved, even after we have been forgiven and made new in Christ, the battle against sin continues. Paul, though a mighty man of God, still wrestled with the reality of his own sinfulness. In Romans 7:19, Paul says, "For the good that I would I do not: but the evil which I would not, that I do." Here, we see the ongoing struggle that every believer faces—the desire to do good, yet the pull of sin that remains in our flesh. Paul's position as the chief of sinners is not just about his past; it is a present reality that reminds us that as long as we live in this fallen world, we will always be in need of God's grace, mercy, and forgiveness. It is a position of humility, of recognizing that without Christ, we are lost, but in Him, we find salvation, hope, and transformation.

The phrase "of whom I am chief" is not just a personal confession for Paul; it is a message of hope for all sinners. If the chief of sinners can be redeemed, then there is no one who is beyond the reach of God's saving power. Paul's life is a testament to the fact that God specializes in saving the worst of the worst. He takes those who are the most broken, the most sinful, and transforms them into vessels of His grace. Paul's position as the chief of sinners magnifies the grace of God, because it shows us that God's love is not limited by the severity of our sin. The chief of sinners is not beyond the grace of God, and neither are we.

In recognizing his position as the chief of sinners, Paul also models for us the kind of humility that should characterize every Christian. The more we understand God's holiness, the more we understand our own sinfulness, and the more grateful we become for His grace. It is only when we take the position of the chief of sinners that we can truly appreciate the depth of God's love for us. When we acknowledge our sinfulness, we are better able to see the incredible mercy that God has shown us through Christ. It is in this position of humility that we can fully embrace the gift of salvation and live lives that are marked by gratitude, not for anything we have done, but for everything that Christ has done for us.

Paul's position as the chief of sinners also serves as a warning against pride and self-righteousness. It reminds us that no matter how far we have come in our walk with God, no matter how much we have grown in our faith, we are still sinners saved by grace. We must never forget that our salvation is not a result of our own goodness or effort, but solely the result of God's grace. When we remember that we are the chief of sinners, we are protected from the temptation to look down on others or to think of ourselves as better than those who are struggling. We are reminded that we are all in the same boat, all in need of the same Savior, and all equally dependent on God's grace.

The phrase "of whom I am chief" also speaks to the radical nature of God's forgiveness. When we truly understand the depth of our sin, we begin to grasp just how amazing God's forgiveness really is. For God to forgive the chief of sinners is an act of incredible grace, and it shows us that His love is not based on our worthiness, but on His character. God's forgiveness is complete, it is total, and it is unconditional. He does not hold our past against us, and He does not keep a record of wrongs. When He forgives, He removes our sins "as far as the east is from the west" (Psalm 103:12). For Paul to say that he is the chief of sinners, yet to know that he is fully forgiven, is a powerful testimony to the overwhelming grace of God.

In conclusion, Paul's statement "of whom I am chief" in 1 Timothy 1:15 is a profound declaration of humility, honesty, and grace. It is a recognition of the depth of our sinfulness, but it is also a testimony to the incredible mercy of God. Paul's position as the chief of sinners is not one of despair, but one of hope, because it points us to the truth that no one is beyond the reach of God's saving power. It reminds us that we are all sinners in need of grace, and it invites us to take the position of humility, acknowledging our sin and embracing the forgiveness that is offered to us through Christ. "Of whom I am chief" is a phrase that calls us to examine our hearts, to recognize our ongoing need for grace, and to live lives that are marked by gratitude for the incredible love that God has shown us. It is a statement that magnifies the grace of God, because it shows us that even the chief of sinners can be saved, and in that truth, we find the greatest hope of all.

Chapter 9 – Proof

"I am chief"—these three words from 1 Timothy 1:15, spoken by the Apostle Paul, carry the weight of deep personal reflection, humility, and an honest admission of his own sinful past. When Paul calls himself the "chief" of sinners, he is not speaking with exaggeration or seeking to draw attention to himself. Rather, he is providing proof of the overwhelming grace of God. Paul's life is living evidence that God's mercy extends even to the worst of sinners, and by calling himself the "chief," Paul presents himself as the ultimate example of how far-reaching the saving power of Christ truly is. When he says, "I am chief," Paul is not just reflecting on his past actions—though they were terrible, as he persecuted the early church, hunted down Christians, and even approved of their deaths, most famously that of Stephen, the first Christian martyr—but he is also pointing to the depth of his heart's transformation. He does not say, "I was the chief of sinners," but "I am chief," signifying that even now, as a saved and redeemed apostle, he still views himself through the lens of his past rebellion against God's holiness. His use of the present tense is crucial here, indicating that despite all his good works, despite his many accomplishments for the Kingdom of God, Paul remains acutely aware of his own sinful nature. His self-awareness serves as a proof that no matter how righteous one may seem after being redeemed, we are all still deeply in need of God's grace every single day. Paul's testimony is proof that God's love is not for the perfect, nor for those who believe they have no sin, but for those who are broken, flawed, and undeserving.

When Paul says "I am chief," he highlights that he considers himself the foremost among sinners, not to glorify his past mistakes, but to underscore the miracle of God's forgiveness. The fact that the man who once fiercely opposed Christ and His followers could be transformed into one of the most influential apostles is a testament to God's redeeming power. Paul's conversion stands as undeniable proof that there is no sin too great for God to forgive, no heart too hard for God to soften, and no life too damaged for God to restore. His life is a beacon of hope to anyone who feels unworthy of God's love, anyone who believes they have gone too far to be saved. Paul, in his humility, shows us that even the "chief" of sinners is not beyond the reach of Christ's saving grace.

In a way, Paul's proclamation of being the "chief" of sinners is an invitation for all of us to reflect on our own sinfulness. It is a call to recognize that before we can truly understand the depth of God's love and grace, we must first come to terms with the gravity of our sin. Paul does not make this statement to elevate his guilt above others, but to offer proof that no one is too far gone. His life serves as living evidence that God's grace is greater than our sin. The proof of God's mercy is not found in the lives of the righteous or those who feel they have it all together; it is found in the lives of those who have been saved from the depths of their own rebellion. Paul's transformation is proof that God is willing and able to save even the worst of sinners.

The words "I am chief" are also a reminder that salvation is not something we earn or deserve. Paul's position as the "chief" of sinners shows us that salvation is a gift of God's grace, given freely to those who humble themselves and acknowledge their need for a Savior. Paul knew that his past actions made him utterly undeserving of God's love, yet God chose to save him, not because of anything Paul had done, but because of His own mercy and grace. This is proof that salvation is not about our own righteousness or good works; it is about God's grace alone. As Ephesians 2:8-9 says, "For by grace are ye saved through faith; and that not of yourselves: it is the gift of God: Not of works, lest any man should boast." Paul's confession of being the chief of sinners reminds us that none of us can boast in our own righteousness, for we are all sinners saved by grace.

"I am chief" also serves as proof that God uses broken people to accomplish His purposes. Paul's life demonstrates that God does not choose the qualified; He qualifies the chosen. Despite his past, despite being the "chief" of sinners, Paul became one of the most influential leaders in the early church, spreading the Gospel to the Gentiles and writing much of the New Testament. His life is proof that God can take even the most unlikely person and use them for His glory. This should be a source of great encouragement for all of us, knowing that our past does not disqualify us from being used by God. In fact, it is often those with the most broken pasts who can be the greatest testimonies of God's redeeming power. Paul's life shows us that God can take the "chief" of sinners and turn them into a vessel of His grace and mercy, a living proof of the power of the Gospel.

Furthermore, Paul's statement "I am chief" is proof that true humility comes from recognizing our own sinfulness. Paul was a man of great knowledge, wisdom, and spiritual authority, yet he never lost sight of his own need for God's grace. He never became proud or self-righteous, but always remained humble, fully aware of the fact that he was a sinner saved by grace. This humility is something that all Christians should strive for. It is easy to become prideful in our accomplishments, to think that we are better than others because of our spiritual growth or our good deeds. But Paul's words remind us that no matter how far we have come, we are still sinners in need of God's grace. We are still utterly dependent on Him for our salvation and for the strength to live lives that honor Him.

"I am chief" also stands as proof that confession is a vital part of the Christian life. Paul did not hide his past or try to cover up his sins. He openly confessed that he was the chief of sinners, and in doing so, he brought glory to God's grace. His confession was not an act of self-pity or shame; it was a proclamation of God's mercy. When we confess our sins, we acknowledge our need for God's forgiveness, and in doing so, we give Him the glory for the work He has done in our lives. Confession is not about wallowing in guilt or shame; it is about bringing our sins into the light so that God's grace can be displayed in our lives. Paul's openness about his past serves as proof that confession leads to freedom and that there is no sin too great for God to forgive.

In conclusion, Paul's statement "I am chief" in 1 Timothy 1:15 is a powerful proof of the grace, mercy, and transformative power of God. It serves as a reminder that no one is beyond the reach of God's love, that salvation is a gift of grace, not something we earn or deserve, and that God can use even the most broken people to accomplish His purposes. Paul's life is proof that God's grace is greater than our sin, that true humility comes from recognizing our own sinfulness, and that confession leads to freedom. When Paul calls himself the "chief" of sinners, he is not making a statement of despair, but a proclamation of hope, because if the chief of sinners can be saved, then there is hope for all of us. His life stands as living proof that God's grace is sufficient, that His mercy is boundless, and that His love reaches even the deepest parts of our brokenness. Through Paul's example, we see that our past does not define us; God's grace does.

And in that truth, we find the greatest hope and assurance that we, too, can be forgiven, redeemed, and transformed by the power of the Gospel.

Chapter 10 – Power

"Christ Jesus came"—these three words in 1 Timothy 1:15 hold within them the immense power of God's love, mercy, and ultimate rescue plan for a lost and broken world. The phrase "Christ Jesus came" is a declaration that shatters the hopelessness of humanity, a bold proclamation that God Himself stepped into our world, intervening in the course of history to bring salvation where there was only sin, death, and separation from Him. The power behind these words is beyond comprehension because they carry the full weight of divine intervention. Christ Jesus didn't just happen upon the scene of history; He came with purpose, intent, and authority. He came as the fulfillment of God's eternal plan of redemption, a plan set in motion before the foundations of the world were laid (Ephesians 1:4). This coming of Christ Jesus wasn't an accident or a reaction to human sin—it was the ultimate display of God's sovereignty and love, and the embodiment of His plan to save humanity from the curse of sin. The power in "Christ Jesus came" is the power of God coming down to meet humanity in our lowest, most helpless state, to lift us out of the mire and into the glorious light of His salvation.

When Paul writes, "Christ Jesus came," he is referring to a deliberate act of God, an act that holds the power to transform lives, to restore broken relationships, to heal, and to redeem. Christ Jesus came not as a distant ruler or a detached deity, but as God in the flesh, fully human and fully divine, who walked among us, ate with us, and ultimately died for us. The power in these words lies in the fact that God did not leave us in our sins; He did not abandon us to the consequences of our rebellion. Instead, He sent His Son to come and dwell among us (John 1:14). This is the power of love in action—love that does not just watch from afar but steps into the mess of our lives, takes on our burdens, and offers us a way out. The incarnation—God becoming man—is the ultimate demonstration of God's power, because it shows us that nothing can separate us from His love. "Christ Jesus came" means that He came to bring light into the darkness, to rescue the lost, to seek and to save that which was broken (Luke 19:10). This coming of Christ was not just a visit or an appearance; it was a mission to redeem and restore. The power of His coming was seen in His birth, His life, His death, and His resurrection.

"Christ Jesus came" with the power to change everything. When He came, He brought with Him the power to forgive sins, to heal the sick, to raise the dead, and to give hope to the hopeless. His coming was the fulfillment of centuries of prophecy, the long-awaited Messiah who would save His people from their sins (Matthew 1:21). The power in these words is the power of salvation itself. Without Christ Jesus coming into the world, we would still be lost, trapped in our sin, without hope and without God. But because He came, everything changed. He came to be the perfect, sinless sacrifice for our sins. He came to live the life we could not live, and to die the death we deserved to die. "Christ Jesus came" means that God made a way where there was no way, that the barrier of sin that separated us from Him was torn down, and that through Christ, we now have access to the Father (Ephesians 2:18). His coming was not just a moment in history—it was the turning point of all history. His coming brought the power of eternal life, the power to reconcile us to God, the power to defeat sin and death once and for all.

"Christ Jesus came" speaks of the power of humility. When He came, He didn't come in the way that people expected. He didn't come as a conquering king or a political leader, but as a baby born in a manger, in the most humble of circumstances (Luke 2:7). The power of His coming is seen in the fact that He laid aside His glory and took on the form of a servant (Philippians 2:7). He humbled Himself, not only in His birth but throughout His life, as He lived in obedience to the Father, even unto death, the death of the cross (Philippians 2:8). The power of Christ Jesus' coming is that He came not to be served, but to serve, and to give His life as a ransom for many (Matthew 20:28). This is the power of sacrificial love, love that goes to the ultimate lengths to save those who are lost. When Christ Jesus came, He showed us the true meaning of power—not power that dominates or controls, but power that lays itself down for the sake of others. This is the power of the Gospel, the power of God's love made manifest in the person of Jesus Christ.

"Christ Jesus came" also signifies the power of His mission. He came with a specific purpose: to save sinners (1 Timothy 1:15). This is the heart of His coming—salvation. Jesus didn't come just to be a good example or a wise teacher, though He was both of those things. He came to do something that no one else could do: to save us from our sins. The power in these words lies in the fact that without Christ's coming, we would still be dead in our trespasses and sins (Ephesians 2:1). But because He came, we have the power to be forgiven, to be made new, to be transformed by His grace. The power of His coming is that it brings new life to all who believe in Him. It brings freedom from the bondage of sin, freedom from guilt and shame, and the promise of eternal life. The power of "Christ Jesus came" is the power of the Gospel, the power to save everyone who believes (Romans 1:16).

Furthermore, "Christ Jesus came" speaks of the power of victory. When Christ came, He came to defeat the works of the devil (1 John 3:8). His coming marked the beginning of the end for Satan's reign of sin and death. Through His life, death, and resurrection, Jesus triumphed over every power of darkness. He disarmed the rulers and authorities and made a public spectacle of them, triumphing over them by the cross (Colossians 2:15). The power in these words is the power of victory over every enemy that stands against God's people. When Christ Jesus came, He came to win the ultimate battle against sin, death, and hell. He came to break the chains of sin that held us captive and to set us free. His coming was not just a temporary fix or a partial victory; it was a complete and final triumph over the forces of evil. The power of "Christ Jesus came" is the power of the resurrection, the power that raised Jesus from the dead and now works in the lives of those who believe in Him (Ephesians 1:19-20). It is the power that guarantees that death is not the end for those who are in Christ, but that we too will be raised to new life with Him.

"Christ Jesus came" also speaks of the power of God's faithfulness. His coming was the fulfillment of every promise God had made throughout the Old Testament. From the moment sin entered the world, God promised a Savior, and in Christ Jesus, that promise was fulfilled. The power in these words is the power of a God who keeps His promises, who does not leave His people in their sin but makes a way for their redemption. When Christ Jesus came, He came as the fulfillment of God's covenant with His people, the promise that He would send a Redeemer to crush the head of the serpent (Genesis 3:15). His coming is proof that God is faithful to His word, that He is a God who saves, and that His love for us is steadfast and unchanging.

In conclusion, "Christ Jesus came" from 1 Timothy 1:15 is a phrase that encapsulates the power of God's love, grace, and redemption. It speaks of a God who did not leave us in our sin but came down to rescue us. It speaks of the power of humility, the power of sacrificial love, and the power of victory over sin and death. It is a declaration of the Gospel's power to save, to transform, and to give new life. "Christ Jesus came" is the foundation of our hope, the proof of God's faithfulness, and the guarantee of our salvation. Because Christ Jesus came, everything has changed. The power of His coming is the power that saves us, keeps us, and promises us eternal life with Him. It is the power of the Gospel, the power of God unto salvation for everyone who believes. "Christ Jesus came"—and in that truth, we find the fullness of God's love, the depth of His grace, and the strength of His redeeming power.

Chapter 11 – Perseverance

"Faithful saying"—these two words in 1 Timothy 1:15 carry a message of unshakable perseverance and the enduring reliability of God's truth in a world full of shifting sand and fleeting promises. When the Apostle Paul introduces the phrase "faithful saying," he is telling us that what we are about to hear is not just an opinion, not just a hope, but a truth that has been proven, tested, and found unmovable. It is a declaration that transcends time, circumstances, and human limitations. In a world where so many promises are broken, where people fail us, and where even our best efforts can fall short, this "faithful saying" stands as a rock, a foundation on which we can build our lives, knowing that it will not fail. The phrase itself breathes life into the weary soul, reminding us that while everything around us may change, God's Word remains the same. This "faithful saying" is a promise that we can hold onto with every fiber of our being, especially in the moments when life feels overwhelming, when trials seem unending, and when it feels like the weight of the world is pressing down on us.

When Paul uses the words "faithful saying," he is speaking about the Gospel—the good news that Christ Jesus came into the world to save sinners. This is the ultimate faithful saying, the truth that is worthy of all acceptation, as Paul puts it. It's not just a fleeting sentiment or a comforting thought; it's a fact rooted in the very character of God. God, who is faithful and true, has made a promise through His Son, Jesus Christ, and that promise is that sinners can be saved. No matter how great our sin, no matter how deep our guilt, no matter how long we have wandered from God, this faithful saying remains: Christ came to save sinners, and that includes each and every one of us. The beauty of this faithful saying is that it does not depend on us. It does not rely on our ability to be perfect, to fix ourselves, or to earn our way back to God. It rests entirely on the faithfulness of God. And because God is faithful, this saying is unchanging, unwavering, and eternally reliable.

This "faithful saying" calls us to persevere in our faith, even when life gets hard. It reminds us that no matter what we face, God's promise stands firm. In moments of doubt, when we question whether we are truly forgiven, whether we are truly loved, whether we are truly saved, this faithful saying gives us the assurance we need. Christ Jesus came into the world to save sinners, and that is a fact. It is a faithful saying that holds true in every situation, in every storm, and in every trial. The word "faithful" here speaks to the reliability of God's Word. When everything else in our lives feels unstable, when relationships fail, when plans fall apart, and when the future seems uncertain, we can hold onto this faithful saying as an anchor for our souls. It tells us that no matter what happens, God's love for us, His plan for our salvation, and His promise of eternal life are sure. This truth does not waver with our emotions or our circumstances; it is as solid and dependable as the God who made it.

"Faithful saying" also speaks to the perseverance required of us as believers. Faith is not always easy, and the Christian life is often marked by trials, challenges, and suffering. There will be times when our faith is tested, when we face difficulties that make us want to give up, when the weight of the world feels like too much to bear. In those moments, this faithful saying calls us to keep going, to persevere, to hold fast to the truth of God's Word, even when it feels like everything is falling apart. Hebrews 10:23 encourages us to "hold fast the profession of our faith without wavering; (for he is faithful that promised)." This faithful saying is the reason we can hold fast, the reason we can keep going even when the road ahead seems impossible. Because God is faithful, we can trust that His promises are true, that He will never leave us nor forsake us (Hebrews 13:5), and that He will carry us through whatever trials we face.

The phrase "faithful saying" also carries with it the idea of consistency. God's faithfulness is not occasional or conditional; it is constant, unchanging, and dependable. Just as God's character never changes, His promises never change. This means that the Gospel, the good news that Christ came to save sinners, is as true today as it was when Paul first wrote these words. The same grace that saved Paul, the "chief of sinners," is available to us today, and it is just as powerful, just as effective, just as life-changing. This faithful saying is not bound by time or circumstance. It is as reliable in the darkest night as it is in the brightest day. It is a truth that we can cling to in every season of life, knowing that God's Word never fails.

In our modern world, where truth often feels relative and shifting, this "faithful saying" stands as a beacon of light. It tells us that there is something we can trust in completely, something that will never change, never falter, never fade. It is the foundation upon which we build our faith, the cornerstone of our hope, and the source of our perseverance. When the storms of life rage, when doubts assail us, when we feel like giving up, this faithful saying reminds us that we are not alone, that God is with us, and that His promises will never fail. This is the truth that sustains us, the truth that gives us strength to keep going, and the truth that reminds us that our salvation is secure in Christ.

Moreover, the phrase "faithful saying" reminds us that God is faithful even when we are not. There will be times when we fall short, when our faith is weak, and when we struggle to hold on. But even in those moments, God remains faithful. 2 Timothy 2:13 tells us, "If we believe not, yet he abideth faithful: he cannot deny himself." God's faithfulness is not dependent on us. His promises are not contingent upon our ability to keep them. Even when we fail, even when we stumble, God's faithfulness endures. This faithful saying, that Christ came to save sinners, stands firm no matter what. It is the anchor that holds us, even when we feel like we are drifting. It is the truth that brings us back, even when we have wandered far.

The power of this "faithful saying" lies not in its simplicity, but in its depth. It speaks to the very heart of God's character—His steadfast love, His unchanging nature, and His commitment to save those who come to Him. It is a faithful saying because it reflects the faithfulness of God. And because God is faithful, we can persevere. We can keep trusting, keep believing, and keep walking forward, knowing that God's promises are true. This faithful saying is the foundation of our perseverance. It gives us the strength to endure hardships, the courage to face challenges, and the hope to keep going, even when life feels overwhelming.

In conclusion, the phrase "faithful saying" in 1 Timothy 1:15 is a powerful reminder of the unchanging, unwavering truth of the Gospel. It calls us to persevere in our faith, knowing that God's promises are true and that His love for us is steadfast. This faithful saying, that Christ Jesus came into the world to save sinners, is the foundation of our hope, the anchor of our souls, and the reason we can keep going, no matter what we face. It is a truth that never changes, a promise that never fails, and a declaration of God's faithfulness that endures through all time. In this faithful saying, we find the strength to persevere, the courage to stand firm, and the assurance that God's grace is sufficient for every trial, every struggle, and every season of life. Because this is a faithful saying, we can rest in the knowledge that God is with us, that His promises are true, and that our salvation is secure in Him.

Chapter 12 – Promise

"Worthy of all acceptation"—these powerful words from 1 Timothy 1:15 hold within them a divine promise that transcends time and circumstance, a truth that is so profound, so life-altering, that it is deserving of our complete, wholehearted acceptance. Paul is not just suggesting this promise to be something we might consider; he is declaring with absolute conviction that this message—this truth of the Gospel—is something that every single person, in every situation, in every corner of the earth, must receive and embrace with open arms. "Worthy of all acceptation" means that this promise of salvation through Christ Jesus is not just a vague hope or a fleeting possibility, but a guaranteed reality for all who will believe. It is a truth that carries eternal weight and significance, so trustworthy and so vital that it demands to be fully accepted by everyone who hears it. This phrase is not a call for partial belief or cautious optimism; it is a call for complete and total surrender to the reality of God's saving grace. The promise contained in these words—that Christ Jesus came into the world to save sinners—is not just another religious teaching or philosophy among many, but the ultimate, unshakable truth that holds the power to transform lives, heal broken hearts, and restore what sin has destroyed.

When Paul says that this promise is "worthy of all acceptation," he is telling us that it is fully dependable, absolutely reliable, and utterly trustworthy. It is a promise that comes directly from the heart of God, who cannot lie, who does not change, and whose love is boundless. This is not the kind of promise that we experience in human relationships—promises that are often broken or unfulfilled due to circumstances, weaknesses, or failures. No, this is a divine promise, made by the Creator of the universe, and sealed with the blood of His Son. It is a promise that cannot be revoked, undone, or altered. It is as certain as the rising of the sun, as sure as the stars in the sky, because it is rooted in the very character of God. When Paul says that it is "worthy of all acceptation," he means that this promise is worthy of being trusted with every fiber of our being, worthy of staking our entire lives upon it, worthy of building our hope, our faith, and our future on its unmovable foundation.

This phrase "worthy of all acceptation" also speaks to the universality of the Gospel. It tells us that this promise is not limited to a specific group of people, a certain class, or a particular culture. It is a promise for all—rich and poor, young and old, the educated and uneducated, the sinner who has lived a life of rebellion and the person who has tried to walk the moral path but still feels empty inside. There is no one who is excluded from this promise. It is worthy of acceptance by all because it is a promise offered to all. John 3:16 reminds us, "For God so loved the world, that he gave his only begotten Son, that whosoever believeth in him should not perish, but have everlasting life." This is the promise that is worthy of all acceptation—the promise that Jesus Christ came into the world to save sinners, and that "whosoever" believes in Him will not perish but will have eternal life. It is an open invitation, extended to every person, no matter their past, their failures, or their doubts.

The promise contained in this phrase is not just about eternal life in the distant future, though that is a glorious part of it. It is also a promise for the here and now. It is a promise of forgiveness, of freedom from guilt and shame, of peace that passes understanding, and of joy that is unshakable even in the midst of life's storms. It is a promise that Christ Jesus came to bring us into a relationship with God, to restore what was lost in the Garden of Eden, to tear down the wall of separation between us and our Creator, and to give us the abundant life that only comes through knowing Him. This promise is worthy of all acceptation because it offers us what nothing else in this world can—true, lasting peace with God. Romans 5:1 declares, "Therefore being justified by faith, we have peace with God through our Lord Jesus Christ." This peace, this reconciliation, this new life in Christ is the heart of the promise that Paul is urging us to accept fully, without reservation, because it is the very thing our souls long for.

"Worthy of all acceptation" means that this promise is not something we should treat casually or indifferently. It is not a message to be placed on a shelf and dusted off when it is convenient. It is a promise that demands our attention, our devotion, and our faith. It is a truth that is so weighty, so magnificent, that it deserves to be the center of our lives, the driving force behind all we do, the foundation upon which we stand. This is the promise that changes everything—the promise that God Himself came down to earth, took on flesh, and gave His life so that we might be saved. It is a promise that offers hope to the hopeless, healing to the broken, and salvation to the lost. It is a promise that brings light into the darkest places, that breathes life into what was once dead, that offers freedom to those who are bound by sin and shame. And because this promise is "worthy of all acceptation," we are called to embrace it fully, to let it sink deep into our hearts, and to live in the light of its truth every single day.

The phrase "worthy of all acceptation" also challenges us to examine the way we respond to this promise. If it is truly worthy of all acceptation, then we must ask ourselves if we are fully accepting it. Have we embraced the fullness of what God has offered us in Christ? Have we accepted not only the forgiveness of our sins, but also the new identity, the new purpose, and the new life that comes with being a child of God? To accept this promise fully means to surrender our lives to the One who gave His life for us. It means to trust Him not only with our salvation but with our every moment, our every decision, our every breath. It means to live in the confidence that His promise is sure, that His grace is sufficient, and that His love will never fail.

"Worthy of all acceptation" is also a reminder that this promise is not just for us individually, but for the world around us. If this promise is truly worthy of all acceptation, then we have a responsibility to share it with others. We cannot keep this life-changing truth to ourselves. The same promise that has brought us peace, joy, and salvation is the promise that the world desperately needs to hear. In a world filled with broken promises, where people are searching for meaning, purpose, and hope, this faithful promise stands as a beacon of light. It is worthy of all acceptation, and it is worthy of being shared with everyone we meet. The Gospel is not just good news for us; it is good news for all. And if we truly believe that this promise is worthy of all acceptation, then we must be willing to proclaim it, to live it out, and to invite others into the life-changing reality of God's grace.

In conclusion, the phrase "worthy of all acceptation" in 1 Timothy 1:15 carries within it the weight of a divine promise that is not only trustworthy but also life-altering. It is a promise that Christ Jesus came into the world to save sinners—a promise that is offered to all, regardless of background, past sins, or present struggles. It is a promise that brings peace with God, forgiveness of sins, and the hope of eternal life. It is a promise that changes everything, a promise that is deserving of our full, wholehearted acceptance. In a world of broken promises and fleeting hopes, this promise stands firm, rooted in the unchanging character of God. It is worthy of all acceptation because it is the ultimate truth, the greatest hope, and the most profound gift that God has given to humanity. As we reflect on these words, may we be reminded that this promise is not only for us but for all, and may we live in the light of its truth, embracing it fully and sharing it boldly with a world in desperate need of the hope that only Christ can offer.

Conclusion

As we come to the close of "The Chief Sinner Meets the Chief Savior—Reflections on 1 Timothy 1:15," we are left with the undeniable truth that no matter how deep into sin we may have fallen, God's grace is deeper still. The story of Paul, who called himself the "chief of sinners," is a reminder that no one is beyond the reach of God's love, and that the power of the Gospel is transformative beyond what we can imagine. But as we reflect on Paul's encounter with the Chief Savior, we are also challenged to consider what it means to continue walking with the Lord in our own lives. The journey of faith does not end when we first meet Christ—it is just the beginning. The same grace that saved Paul, and the same grace that saved us, is the grace that must guide us each day. To continue in our walk with the Lord means to live in the light of that grace, constantly reminded of our dependence on Christ and the incredible mercy that He has shown us. It means walking in humility, recognizing that we are still sinners saved by grace, and that without Him, we can do nothing. Paul's life after his conversion was marked by perseverance, faithfulness, and a deep desire to spread the message of Jesus to all who would listen. We are called to do the same. We are called to live out our faith boldly, to share the Gospel with those around us, and to let our lives be a reflection of the grace we have received. But this walk is not without its challenges. There will be times when we stumble, when we face trials, and when our faith is tested. In those moments, we must remember the faithful saying that Paul clung to: "Christ Jesus came into the world to save sinners." This is the foundation of our hope, and it is what keeps us grounded in the midst of life's storms. To continue in our walk with the Lord, we must remain anchored in His Word, seeking Him daily in prayer, and trusting Him in all things. We must remember that the same Savior who met us in our brokenness continues to walk with us in our struggles, offering His strength, His peace, and His grace. As we move forward in our faith, let us be mindful of the example Paul set—an example of humility, perseverance, and relentless trust in the Lord. Let us never forget that we, too, were once sinners in need of saving, and that it is by God's grace alone that we are able to walk this path. As we continue in our journey, may we do so with hearts full of gratitude, hands ready to serve, and lives that reflect the love and mercy of the One who saved us. In our walk with the Lord, may we continually be drawn closer to Him, growing in our faith, and leading others to the Chief Savior who is always ready to meet the chief of sinners and bring them into the fullness of His love and grace.

Don't miss out!

Visit the website below and you can sign up to receive emails whenever Joshua Rhoades publishes a new book. There's no charge and no obligation.

https://books2read.com/r/B-A-AJLBB-BQECF

BOOKS 2 READ

Connecting independent readers to independent writers.

Did you love *The Chief Sinner Meets The Chief Saviour Reflections On I Timothy 1:15*? Then you should read *From Brokenness To Beauty Written By The Pen of Grace*[1] by Joshua Rhoades!

From Brokenness to Beauty: Written by the Pen of Grace is a profound journey into the heart of God's redemptive love. In a world where we often carry the weight of our brokenness—whether from personal mistakes, life's unexpected hardships, or the deep pain caused by others—this book serves as a beacon of hope. It reminds us that no matter how shattered we may feel, God's grace can transform our pain into something beautiful, rewriting the story of our lives with His endless love.

We all face moments when we feel lost, unsure of where to turn, burdened by regrets, and unsure of how to move forward. But God's grace is not just a comforting idea; it is the very force of His love, ever-present and powerful, working even in the messiest parts of our lives. Grace doesn't erase the past—it redeems it. Through every failure, every tear, every moment of despair, God's

---

1. https://books2read.com/u/47BJKN

2. https://books2read.com/u/47BJKN

grace is at work, taking what seems beyond repair and molding it into something greater than we could ever imagine.

This book invites you to see your brokenness through the eyes of grace, to trust that God is not finished with you yet, and to believe that no matter how incomplete or painful your story may seem, He is still writing it. In these pages, you'll discover that God uses the hardest chapters of our lives to showcase His love and healing. Let this be the start of your journey from brokenness to beauty, as you allow the loving hand of God's grace to rewrite your life into a testimony of His unending faithfulness.